Deanna
Always Keep
giving to others
God Bless
Cyn

The Whisper

A Guide to help Educate and Support Individuals Dealing with the Dying Process of a Loved One

By

Cynthia Swift

ISBN 0-7414-3660-4

Published by:

INFINITY
PUBLISHING.COM

1094 New DeHaven Street, Suite 100
West Conshohocken, PA 19428-2713
Info@buybooksontheweb.com
www.buybooksontheweb.com
Toll-free (877) BUY BOOK
Local Phone (610) 941-9999
Fax (610) 941-9959

Printed in the United States of America

Printed on Recycled Paper

Published February 2007

This book is dedicated in memory of
My Mother and Best Friend

Arlene Swift-Archey
May 22, 1930 – December 23, 1986

Contents

The Whisper

Introduction

The book you are holding, has been given to you, or you have selected it for a reason. Most likely you are on, or beginning a journey filled with stress and emotional pain. At the end, you will experience the loss of a special person. It will be difficult, but you ***will*** get through it. For many of you, it will be a time of coming together as a family, with the nucleus being your loved one in the process of dying. It may be a time of healing broken relationships, and supporting those around you. Maybe it will be resolving or healing something within yourself, discovering an inner strength deep inside, you never knew existed. It may be a time to let go of bitterness or resentment, ask to be forgiven or to forgive. Sometimes, that includes forgiving *ourselves.* It is a time to strive to have a greater understanding of life by putting things in perspective. To realize what is truly important, thus cherishing and accepting all God has given us… the good and the bad. As you begin this journey for the first time, or if you have experienced it before, take time to support and nurture each other. Respect one another's way of coping or dealing with the loss of this special person and the relationship they share. Take care of yourself physically, emotionally and spiritually. Allow yourself to grow as a person…. celebrate ***life.***

For many of us, there is an unsettling time between our knowledge of, and / or realization, regarding the downward spiral of a loved one. A time when we have to accept there will no longer be a resurgence or recovery. It is a time of questioning, as we wrestle with our heart, mind and spirit. A time to decide, will it be "***quality*** or ***quantity,***" and remind ourselves there's a big difference between the two.

Do we just "give up" on our loved one, or continue a hopeless battle for a little more time? We must honestly ask ourselves, "is the extra time for ***them*** or for ***me?***" and decide if the pain this person may have to endure physically, mentally, emotionally and spiritually, worth the added hours, days or months it ***may*** add to their life. We must ask ourselves if we love this person enough to ***let go*** and allow Hospice or a Palliative Care team come in and take over. Are we able to let go of the reigns of control enough to let them come in and make life-changing decisions? Some that may allow the end to come sooner by providing comfort in a spiritually safe, loving environment, and medications given to provide freedom from pain.

The time spent prior to making the decision to call Hospice or an End of Life Care team is life changing for many people. Some feel enormous ***guilt*** equating this specialized care with "giving up or throwing in the towel" where their loved one is concerned. Many feel ***anger*** toward the Medical Society, the disease, and even toward the person facing death. Some feel ***fear***. The fear of living without this person, or facing our own mortality. All of these feelings are normal. It is okay to have and feel them. The most difficult question we must ask is, "do I love this person enough to "hand them over?" When that time comes, and you let go of the control and decision making, allow yourself to love and support your loved one in the dying process. Respect their wishes even if sometimes you don't understand *why* they want something a certain way, or it may make you feel uncomfortable. It's not about ***you***, it's about them and what ***they*** want and need. At times, it can be extremely difficult, but this is not a rehearsal. We can't go back in time and do it over, and we don't want to regret anything. By loving, respecting and accepting this person through the dying process, it will help us love, respect and accept ***ourselves*** when it's over.

When faced with the decision to call an End of Life Care team or Hospice, educate yourself. Ask questions of experienced caregivers trained in this kind of nursing. Seek spiritual guidance, and accept whatever help is available to get you through this difficult time. After the decision is made, make the most of the time that remains. Rejoice and celebrate the life of this special person now in the process of leaving this world. Give thanks for the blessings you have received from them. Say ***everything*** you need and want to say, don't hold back. If you feel the need, ask for their forgiveness, or forgive them. Tell them you love them…you will miss them. Take advantage of the precious gift of time you have been given and remember, "it is not good-bye, it's till we meet again."

Death, the final frontier, or is it? Many of us fear this last stage of life because it is "unknown," and since most of us have never had a near death experience, we really don't know what to expect.

As a Hospice nurse, I have the opportunity and honor of sharing in the last stages of life with patients and their families. During this time, I am blessed, as they take me under their wing, close to their heart and carry me along on their journey from life to death. These unique individuals have been, and continue to be extraordinary teachers.

Dying is a "group" experience. It doesn't just happen to the patient, it spills over to envelop family, friends and those caring for this special person. It affects ***everyone***.

In this booklet, I will do my best to help you know what to expect. Education helps to reduce fear, and no one likes to be taken "off guard," therefore if we have an idea of what ***may*** happen next, we are better able to prepare.

As you read on, you will discover I am very deeply rooted in my spiritual beliefs and faith. I am a Christian. I believe that is ***why*** I am able to do what I do day after day. I also know, not everyone's religious beliefs are the same as mine and I respect that.

I don't believe death is a ***bad*** thing, and from what I've witnessed and learned, it is not the end.

Actually, I see it as a "present or reward" for a job well done. It is the beginning of something so glorious we can only imagine it in our hearts and minds. None of us get out of this alive. God did not create our ***physical*** bodies to live forever. The time we spend here on earth is a learning time. A time to do a job we were sent here to do. To touch lives, love and serve God. When all is done, we will hear a gentle whisper saying, "well done good and faithful servant" and a door will open to love, light, joy and a reunion with those that have gone before us.

Because of my privilege of working with the dying, I can honestly say I have no fear of death. I have been taught well and thank all my "teachers" in the past, present, and those to come.

Everyone is unique. Therefore, each dying experience is unique. A person dies in their own time, and the time God has chosen for them.

In the following pages, I will do my best to give an approximate timeline of the dying process and what may or may not happen. Remember, each person is different therefore not everyone will do ***what*** I describe, or in the order described. Some may skip a step. Some may progress then digress in the dying process. This is only an outline. For many, the dying process will begin months before the last breath is taken. For others it may only be minutes.

As human beings, we are a miracle in ourselves. We are “spiritual beings” with so much going on ***inside*** others can’t see. Because of this, it is very easy for loved ones to forget the person in the dying process is doing a lot of internal preparation. For them (the patient) to be able to complete this task, they must and ***need*** to distance themselves from the outside world. This can sometimes be extremely difficult for loved ones to accept and deal with.

When working with families, I like to use the analogy of our bodies being like a car. We are human “machines” made up of “systems.” As one system tires and slows, another will begin to work harder to compensate and keep up. By doing so, the body gives us as caregivers, clues or physical signs that changes are taking place. As we observe these changes, it gives us the information needed to provide comfort through medications to relieve pain along with other comfort measures such as body repositioning, applying cool compresses, or giving oral care to keep the mouth moist. We also tune in to the signs and symptoms of emotional and spiritual needs of the patient and family, and do our best to fulfill those needs.

Location

The place one chooses to take their last breath and the reason that place is chosen is extremely important for a number of reasons. We have already determined the dying process is a very personal thing. Therefore, the place one chooses has significance. Long ago, most everyone died in their own home in their own bed, or that of a close relative. In those days doctors made house calls, if a doctor was even involved. Today, a person has a number of options as to where they choose to die.

Because of the soaring costs in medical care, hospitals do not keep patients any longer than absolutely necessary. Where patients would stay 7-10 days after a surgery, they are now discharged in half the time, and new mothers go home 24-36 hours after giving birth. Staying in the hospital to die is no longer an option. Because of the demand for Hospice or Palliative Care, hospitals are starting to create "specialty units" within their facility to provide this kind of nursing. Some patients may be transferred directly to the specialty unit from an acute unit if they have been given a diagnosis that is terminal and nursing care is needed. Some patients may be admitted from the outside. For someone to qualify for Hospice or a Palliative Care program, they will usually need a "Certificate of Terminal Illness" signed by a doctor stating they have a prognosis of 6 months or less to live. Many facilities will also require some kind of referral.

While nursing care in a specialty unit within the hospital can be excellent, it still takes on the ***feeling*** of a medical institution because of its location. Some patients and their loved ones choose not to have that ***clinical*** environment in the last days.

Option #2 is a Residential Hospice. This is a facility with a limited number of beds mostly private, with some semi-private for insurance reasons. The low number of beds is a plus when looking at nurse and nursing assistant to patient ratio, but also makes a facility such as this harder to get into. The care is exceptional for the patient as well as the family. From my experience, I have found the Residential Hospice to be the most home-like environment. In addition to the skilled nursing care, there almost always is a full-time clergy on site along with counselors for adults as well as children to assist and support loved ones through this difficult time. Many facilities have external programs in place such as children's camps and survivor support groups. Most counselors will follow surviving family members or a loved one up to a year after the death. The physical structure of the facility is home like, inviting and comforting. The "suites" are set up to encourage family and loved ones to participate or be included in this last stage of life. They are large, with a sofa sleeper and usually a small dinette set and recliner.

The bathrooms are spacious and staff will encourage family to stay and use the suite like a mini apartment. The bed linen will usually be found to be a soothing color or print, not hospital white and the bed is usually topped off with a quilt or comforter. The room is more like a beautiful hotel room rather than a hospital. Families will usually have access to a kitchen complete with everything needed to cook and serve a home made meal and are encouraged to cook for themselves and their loved one if they feel like eating. Working as a nurse in a facility such as this, I found it to be extremely healing for everyone involved, with the staff in tune to the needs and wants of the patient and family. By working so closely with families, staff can identify the need for spiritual and emotional support and immediately put them in touch with the appropriate support person.

I would like to share a story with you from an experience I had while working in a residential hospice. A young woman about the age of 45, married, with two high school age boys was admitted to our facility with end stage liver cancer. "Barb" and her husband were both teachers. She taught music at a high school, while her husband taught at one of the local universities. They had just finished the final decorating of their "dream house" prior to her being diagnosed and given less than six months to live. One day I sat down and asked Barb *why* she had chosen to come to the residence rather than have home care hospice. I wanted to know why she left a ***home*** she dearly loved and had mentioned several times she had not wanted to leave. Her response was, "I love my boys." Barb shared she would have loved to have stayed and passed in the home she enjoyed so much, but didn't want her boys to have to ***live*** in the place she ***died***. She ***knew*** them and didn't want them to carry that memory. She wanted their home to be a place of joy, comfort and a safe refuge. She felt by serving herself, and staying home to die, that joy and comfort would be taken away. I think Barb made the right choice for her situation.

Option #3 Dying at Home. This is a very personal thing. For some people facing death and the families that support them, it's a no brainer. They would never think of leaving their home to go somewhere else to die. Some family members find great comfort in being able to look in a room, or at a bed and remember someone they loved died there. It helps keep them connected in some way, and from that they receive comfort. It goes back to the beginning of the book reminding us we are all different and unique. If someone chooses to die at home, there are many home care and home hospice agencies available to help the family give care and receive support throughout the dying process. Family members are taught how to administer medications for pain and always have someone a phone call away if assistance is needed.

Option #4 Nursing Home or Extended Care facility. Many people will die in a facility such as this because they have been a resident there for years, and it is like dying at home. More and more extended care facilities are creating units for those residents that are in their last days with cancer, dementia or just old age. The needs of a person change when they get to the end of life, therefore the environment and nursing care need to change with them. Pain issues and comfort care are at the top of the list to be addressed. The family will need support during this time thus utilizing the expertise of the clergy and social worker in addition to nursing. It is important the doctor or medical director be on the same page as the nursing staff to be able to provide the appropriate care needed at this time. For families who have had a parent or spouse in a facility for a long time, they tend to think of caregivers and staff as family, which can be a great source of comfort and support. It also is important for the staff to be able to communicate their needs, and seek support for themselves when caring for someone that has become a part of their lives as well.

The options are there. It is important that end of life care and where it will take place be discussed at the earliest possible time. All fears, wants and concerns should be put on the table and be open for discussion.

Remember dying is a ***group*** experience, and being able to discuss what is going to happen and decide how things will be handled can take an enormous stress or load off everyone. This also includes discussing and making all funeral arrangements ahead of time. Some families find it helpful to assign each family member or loved one a designated or specific responsibility/task. If children are old enough, and express the need or desire to be included, by all means allow them that role. Many children and/or grandchildren will harbor anger and/or resentment if their need to contribute is denied. By feeling included, and being an active part of the planning, you are allowing them to start their own grieving process. Many children, even those that are very young, may feel the need to share their feelings and be allowed to verbalize them. You may want to ask the young person if they would like to share a poem or special memory thus opening a door for them to express what they are feeling. Always make yourself available to them. If you feel you are not able to handle this supportive role for whatever reason, ask a favorite adult to step in for you to lend an open ear and give needed support and understanding.

Pain Control

My number one priority as a patient advocate is pain control. This is a huge issue and can be a great source of fear and apprehension. Because of this, pain is addressed in the very beginning as I start educating and building a special relationship with my patient and their loved ones. Trust is an issue for everyone concerned and a clear understanding of what the patient expects from me regarding pain control is a must. With all the medications we have available to us in today's world, there is no reason for anyone to die in pain. *Everyone* is entitled to a good death, with dignity and as much comfort as can be given in every area. The question I ask my patients early in our relationship is "if the pain gets to be too much, do you want to be sedated, or would you like enough medication to relieve as much pain as possible, and allow you to remain conscious." Most everyone will tell me they want to be sedated. By this time, they have said their goodbyes to family and friends, and need the reassurance they will be kept from suffering. The simple fact they can trust me to keep them comfortable, is a huge relief for the person in the process of dying. Taking away the fear of having to endure great pain at the end of ones life, frees them to make what time is left happy and productive. It takes away anxiety. I suggest early on, the patient have a clear understanding with their family and loved ones regarding what they (the patient) have requested for end of life pain control. That way there will be no confusion or animosity on the part of the family toward nursing staff when, and if the time comes to put into play the request regarding pain control and sedation.

All pain control options should be discussed early on, including the way the medication will be delivered such as through patches, injections, orally or rectally. Side effects like hallucinations, constipation and nausea etc. should also be addressed. Education is a key priority. It is very important for all those involved in the care and support of the patient know when they (the patient) complain of pain, it is *not* our place to determine *if* pain is present, or how *much* pain they are experiencing. Pain is whatever the patient says it is, and should be addressed...period.

There are combinations of medications that can be given to treat pain and agitation. Many of these medications also provide some respiratory relief, and can be delivered in several ways. Any and all medications and their uses should be discussed. You must remember what works well for one person, may not work well for someone else. Sometimes in the beginning, it's trial and error to find something that gives good relief. From there, the dose and frequency can be fine tuned to give maximum comfort. Because of the use of narcotics, constipation is a direct side effect for most people. When you add narcotics for pain control to the already decreased fluid intake and lack of physical activity, you have a perfect setup for constipation. Usually at this stage, the patient is eating bites, if anything, but the body still needs to rid itself of waste. The nursing staff will keep careful track of bowel activity and will take appropriate action. There are several medications that work well when given orally, along with special food preps designed specifically for constipation. If needed, a suppository or enema can be given.

Timeline

Approximately
One to Three
Months Prior to Passing

Withdrawal

As the realization of dying is processed and accepted by the patient, it becomes real. Most are able to verbalize, "I am dying," and many have the ***need*** to talk about it. Once this is established, the person will begin to withdraw or start to separate themselves from the world around them. They will usually lose interest in T.V., newspapers, other media, and current events. Next will be the separation from people, even those most loved and cherished by the patient. This time can be extremely difficult and painful for loved ones because it is usually taken "personally." Loved ones will ask questions like, "don't they love me as much as I love them? Don't they want to stay here with us as long as they can? Are they angry or upset with me for some reason?" Most loved ones will have questions such as the ones I mentioned, but many will never verbalize them. For those of you that will be left behind, please know it is natural and very normal to cling to, and feel the need for closeness with our loved one in the process of passing, but we must not confuse ***our*** needs with the needs and work that must be done by the patient. It is not you, or anything you did or did not do. It ***is*** part of the dying process.

During this time, a person will begin to sleep more, with an extra nap here and there. During the "sleep time," a lot is going on that we don't see. The person is evaluating themselves and their life, ***sorting*** things out and taking care of business. This is something the person must do alone, and as hard as it is, we must respect this. Verbal communication will decrease and words are not as important as before. Now, the human touch and eye contact take on much more meaning.

Food

Food is a life sustaining need. We use it to nourish, repair, and give our bodies strength and energy. As the body prepares to die, it no longer needs food. This is one of the hardest areas for loved ones to understand and accept. Our whole lives, we have been taught to equate food with health, comfort and love.

The patient's appetite naturally decreases and "nothing tastes good." Occasionally cravings may come and go and unless the person is not able to swallow without choking, they should be able to eat whatever they desire. Eventually, they will only be able to accept liquids, and after a while, not even that. It is okay not to eat. The patient should not be forced, or be made to feel guilty for not accepting what is being offered to fulfill the needs of a loved one. From this time on, the energy that is needed is "Spiritual." The Spiritual energy will take over the physical.

It is important to remember when fluids are no longer taken it is a great comfort to the patient to have the mouth swabbed with a moist toothette. Sometimes a small amount of mouthwash can be added to the water, followed by a thin coating of vegetable oil applied to the inside of the mouth with a swab helping to seal in the moisture. There are also a number of oral treatments available to help keep the mouth moist. These can be provided and kept at the bedside to be used by nursing or family as needed for comfort. A lip balm or moisturizer is also soothing.

Many people have a preconceived notion of what happens regarding dehydration, believing it is a very painful way to die. This is not true. Studies have been done indicating that it is just the opposite. When the body is well hydrated, our nerve endings and pain receptors are more sensitive. As dehydration occurs, the pain receptors become dull and are not as sensitive to the message being sent to the brain that pain is present. It has also been proven a dehydrated person does not die sooner than a person that is hydrated. In fact, some have survived several days longer than those receiving I.V. therapy. Dehydration is a natural part of the dying process.

One to Two Weeks Prior to Passing

Most of the time is now spent sleeping. While many can still be awakened, they find it difficult to keep their eyes open for any length of time, and will most likely show signs of confusion or disorientation. It is around this time many patients may begin to talk to people we don't see, and it's almost always someone that has already passed. It is important to know, the person in the dying process, see and hear things we don't. During this time, it is sometimes difficult for loved ones to step out on faith and accept this is not always confusion or hallucinations, but a sequence in a Spiritual process.

I had a unique experience with a patient of mine several years ago. "Judy" was a woman in her late forties dying with lung cancer. She had never been married, had one brother, and both parents were still alive. One morning I walked into her room at the start of my shift, greeting her with "Hi Jude, how ya doin today?" With a smile she replied, "I had some visitors last night." "Really, that's great, friends or relatives?" I asked. "I don't know, I didn't recognize any of them. They were coming in and out of that door over there," as she pointed to the outside corner of the room. A little puzzled I said with a chuckle, "Jude, there isn't a door there." "I know!" she said with amazement, and went on to tell me, all night long she witnessed adults and children quietly come in and out of the "door." When I asked her how she felt about what happened or if it frightened her, she told me it did just the opposite. She shared with me that it gave her a feeling of comfort, and not being alone. "I know there is something on the other side of that door," she said with a smile. Judy was not under the sedating affect of narcotics at the time and was very capable of carrying on a very sane and logical conversation. About a month after her experience, Judy went peacefully through the door.

Surge of Energy

Sometimes, the person in the process of dying will experience a burst or surge of energy. They will suddenly talk clearly and be alert when previously they had been confused, and or lethargic. They may ask to have a favorite meal and actually eat it. They may ask to get up in a chair or be taken outside for a nice walk or sit and visit, when before all they wanted to do was withdraw or sleep. This "last rally" can sometimes bring false hope to loved ones especially if they are unaware this is a common occurrence at the end of ones life. It may also bring false hope if in the past the patient had pulled through an illness when the doctor had prepared the family for the worst. Many times, the person will take this opportunity of clarity to verbalize feelings, share loving thoughts, or say "goodbye." The Spirit is taking over at this time and making last preparations for the final transition. Remember, everyone is different. What I described in the "burst of energy" can come in all levels of intensity. Sometimes it can be so subtle, loved ones didn't recognize it at the time, but when they think back over the series of events after all is said and done, a rally will be recognized no matter how small.

I would like to share an example with you. I cared for a man that had a history of several strokes and end stage Parkinson's disease. He was only able to mumble a few small words and lived everyday with a stiff, contracted body. He had not been able to straighten his legs or arms for over a year, yet continued to have a gentle, loving way about him. He was also blessed to have a wife that was devoted and very much in love with her husband "Hugh." Like clockwork, Jean would come in everyday at lunch to feed and visit with the love of her life. I remember how it brought me to tears as I watched her gently hold his hand, and gaze into his eyes. You could *feel* the love. Hugh would sit in his wheelchair with a distant look, taking the bites of food she offered as she quietly spoke to him. One morning as the aides readied Hugh for the day, they noticed he was *different*. He was smiling and more alert. His body was not as rigid, and he was trying to speak. When Jean came in for lunch, she noticed a change the minute she looked at him. After a wonderful visit, Jean came to me and asked, "Cyn, what is happening?" As her eyes danced with happiness she continued, "he smiled, really smiled at me, and when I held his hand and looked into his eyes, he actually looked back at me like he use to. He even tried to uncross his legs himself! What is happening? Do you think he may be getting better?" I smiled as I gently put my hand on hers and replied, "Jean, all I can tell you is, take this time you have been given and make the most of it. Don't question how or why it's happening, just embrace it." As she walked out the door, I turned to one of the nurses and said, "Hugh is going to die soon." Over the next several days, I watched the two "love birds" and witnessed the blessing they had both received. Jean made the most of her visits staying until it was time to get Hugh ready for bed. She seized the opportunity to gaze lovingly into her husband's eyes and feel him gazing back one last time, like they had done all those years before Hugh's illness robbed them of that life together. About a week after this episode, Huge took a major turn and slipped into a coma. He died with Jean, his loving wife at his bedside. Hugh had his surge, and his wife and family were able to enjoy that time. If it had not been for that "last rally," I may not have picked up on the fact Hugh was going to die much sooner than anyone expected.

Terminal Restlessness

Terminal restlessness is a term given when someone becomes anxious or agitated. The patient will usually move about in bed. Many will "pick" at clothing, bed linen or even the air and appear very busy. Loved ones sometimes take this as a sign the patient is in need of something and will attempt to assist them such as smoothing the bed linen, putting a blanket on or off, or rearranging pillows. Many times the family member will attempt to hold their hand or distract them with a memory, story or song. Unfortunately, attempts are almost always unsuccessful thus causing anxiety and a feeling of failure to the one trying to calm. Some loved ones may assume, or take this as a sign the patient may not want them at the bedside, but this is not the case. Terminal restlessness is part of the dying process. More times than not, the patient will be observed lifting their arms with outstretched hands toward the sky. This may or may not be accompanied by an intent stare as they appear to be concentrating or focusing on something we don't see. It is at this time in the dying process, that the patient is beginning a transition from this world to the next. Some literally have a "foot in both worlds." They are now focusing and looking at what is to come.

Physical Changes

Physical changes will appear as the body begins to lose the ability to maintain itself. Blood pressure will often lower. The heartbeat will increase to as much as 160 beats or more a minute, or may greatly decrease. Usually, the heartbeat will be "***bounding***" (beating harder) in an attempt to keep things going.

The body temperature may become very high, sometimes as high as 105 degrees or more. At this stage, medications such as Tylenol will not affect or reduce body temperature. To help provide comfort, cool compresses can be applied to the forehead and ice packs can be wrapped in washcloths and placed in the armpits, behind the knees, and in the bends of the elbows. During this time, it is not unusual to see perspiration with clamminess. Sometimes, instead of a temperature increase, it may greatly decrease.

Since the body temperature has a direct effect on the body, skin color most likely will also change. Some patients will become flushed because of the increased body temperature, while others will take on a bluish tone with a low body temperature. Along with body temperature, circulation plays a major part in the change of skin tone. Since the heart can no longer effectively distribute blood to the extremities, they will become cold and take on a purple color. This is called "mottling." Because the feet and legs are the furthest from the heart, it usually starts on the bottom of the feet and toes. From there, it will usually progress into the knees, thighs and trunk of the body. The hands will become cool with the nail beds taking on a bluish or "cyanotic" color. There may also be discoloration around the mouth.

Breathing

Significant breathing changes usually occur at this time. Respirations may increase from a normal rate of 16-20 breaths a minute, to 40 or more, or may decrease to as little as 4-6 breaths a minute. Sometimes the patient will breathe in a "blowing" or "puffing" of the lips while exhaling. This is known as "fish breathing." More likely than not, there will be an actual stop of respirations lasting several seconds at the onset, then respirations will resume. This is called "apnea" or the momentary cessation of respirations. In the beginning, this usually starts during sleep times. As the dying process progresses, periods of apnea will become more frequent and last for longer periods of time, sometimes for 30 seconds or more.

Because of the body's natural slowing process, fluid cannot be pumped out as it was before. The renal system or kidneys are shutting down resulting in a decrease in urinary output. The urine passed, if any, will be very dark and concentrated. A collection of fluid, or swelling may be seen in the extremities. This is known as "edema." Because the body is slowing down and not working effectively, the lungs are not able to expand properly to move the oxygen needed to keep them clear. Because of this decrease in lung capacity, fluid will begin to build within the lungs causing congestion. Most of the time, this congestion creates a moist ***rattling or gurgling*** noise sometimes referred to as the "death rattle." It can become very loud at times and may be unsettling for loved ones to listen to. The ***rattle*** may come and go with the breathing pattern fluctuating between congestion with erratic respirations, and a normal breathing pattern. This may also be influenced by the body position. One of the medications used at this time to help with excessive secretions is called a "scope patch" that is usually placed behind the patient's ear, or given in injection form. Another medication used for excessive secretions, is Levsin drops, and can be given sub-lingual (under the tongue).

One to Two Days Prior to Passing

The signs that were present at one to two weeks become more intense, such as increased confusion, as death approaches. Breathing becomes more irregular and will often stop for 10-45 seconds or more, then resume. Congestion will usually increase and become very loud. The breathing pattern along with congestion can and will usually change, especially when the body position is changed. The congestion may temporarily clear, only to quickly return. At this time, all breathing is done through the mouth, making oxygen delivered through a nasal cannula basically ineffective. By continuing the oxygen through the nose, the nasal passages will become dry along with the inside of the mouth, requiring more frequent oral care. Families may still choose to continue the oxygen for "comfort measures" if it makes them feel more comfortable, and this is fine.

The hands and feet will usually become mottled, (a purple like marbling of the skin) and feel cool to the touch. By this time, the mottling will most likely have started working its way up the legs. More times than not, the patient will have become unresponsive to their surroundings, but that does not mean they are unable to hear what is being said, or music that is being played. Usually, the eyes will be slightly open with a glazed appearance. Frequently a tear or tears will be seen gently rolling down the patient's cheek. This is not due to sadness or pain, but a natural occurrence.

Over the years, I have come to learn, most people will approach their death the same way they approached life. Are they generally fearful or insecure? Are they the type of person to never take risks, or are they confident and strong in themselves and beliefs? Most people will die the way they lived.

Two of the biggest reasons for resisting death are unfinished business and fear. Sometimes a person may linger because they are waiting to see or hear from someone. Sometimes the fear is for the loved ones they are leaving behind, concerned for their welfare and ability to go on after the patient is gone. It is at this time, the family or loved one must do a very difficult, unselfish and loving thing. They need to give the dying person "permission" to go. An example; "It's okay Mom. I love you and I'll miss you, but I'll be okay. Do what you need to do…go." Sometimes, that's all it takes. It removes an enormous burden from the shoulders of the dying, replacing it with a feeling of relief and peace.

I would like to take this opportunity to address a situation that sometimes happens and causes great pain, confusion, and grief. Sometimes, the person approaching death has decided to do it ***alone***, without anyone present. This can cause great conflict and emotional distress for family members, especially if they want to be present at the moment their loved one passes. But as stated earlier, this is not about the family members or loved ones this is about the person that is passing and what ***their need*** may be for whatever reason. It is a very personal thing, this "business of dying."

I cared for a young woman in her late thirties with breast cancer that had spread to the lungs. "Tina" was divorced with a teenage daughter. Her parents were very devoted, loving, and participated in Tina's care. As it grew closer to the end, someone was in the room at all times. If one family member needed a break, another was ready to take their place at the bedside. This vigil went on for days. As the family became more exhausted, their coping skills began to deteriorate. They became anxious and emotionally fragile. The questions of "when will this be over?" and "how long can this go on?" was asked over and over. Several of us that cared for Tina talked and came to the conclusion that Tina was going to do this alone. Maybe Tina would feel she was deserting her daughter if she was present when she passed. We quietly entered the room and suggested to the family they all take a break together. One of the staff offered to bring coffee and snacks to the cozy sitting area next to the fireplace in the dining room, and the family agreed. Quietly they left the room one at a time, each looking back as they walked out the door. They were not gone more than two or three minutes and Tina passed.

She was waiting for them to leave. Some patients want to spare their loved ones the pain of watching. Some feel they will be deserting their loved ones if they die when they are present. Some just want it to be between them and Jesus. It is a very personal thing.

Family members and loved ones will ask as death approaches if it is okay or ***safe*** to go out for a cup of coffee or go home to take a quick shower. Some will ask if it's safe to go home and sleep in their own bed, especially if they have been at the bedside for a long period of time and there has been no significant change. Just sitting and waiting can be extremely draining and exhausting on our bodies in many different ways. We must all remind ourselves death does not come in our time. It comes at the time God chooses. The nurses may be able to give you a ballpark figure of when we ***think*** it may be, by what the body is telling us, but none of us know for sure. Use your gut instinct. What I ask my families when they bring the subject up is, "what are you able to live with?" For example, you want to be present at the time of death and have faithfully stayed by the bedside for hours or days with no significant change. You need a break, shower, whatever, and you decide to leave for a while. If that person passes while you are gone, will you be okay? Can you live with that and not beat yourself up over it in the days that follow? Did you say your goodbyes and feel confident in the fact that your loved one knew you loved them and wanted to be by their side at the end? If you answered "yes" to these questions, be assured your loved ones death happened the way it was suppose to. Do not feel guilty about not being present, feel you let them down, or are a bad person for "not sticking it out no matter what." Sometimes, it's just not meant to be.

Many families will take this "waiting time" to share favorite scriptures or read a favorite book, poems or stories out loud. This can be a great source of comfort for everyone. Music is also very powerful and soothing. Most families will bring in favorites of the patient. These may include, old hymns, polish polka music, classical or rock. If you don't have a small stereo, most facilities will provide one for you to use. It has been proven the last sense to leave the body is the ability to hear. ***Always*** take advantage of this very special gift God has given us by telling your loved one anything and everything you want and need to say.

When the last breath is taken, the eyes may open wide and a grimace may come to the face. Sometimes it may look like the person is experiencing pain, but it is actually due to the involuntary muscles in the face and chemical changes in the body. Even so, it can be disturbing to those present.

When the heart ceases to beat and the lungs no longer move air, the "machine" stops…but the Spirit lives on. Our loved one sheds the "earth suit" that has served them over the years and meets Jesus at the doors of heaven. There is no longer pain or sadness, only joy.

After Passing

The nurse will need to be called if not present at the time, to confirm your loved one has passed and determine the time of death. This information is needed for legal purposes. You may stay and spend time alone in your loved ones room after their passing if desired. There is no rush to do anything. You must be aware however, there will continue to be physical changes that may take place. Involuntary muscles will continue to slow down and may produce some delayed movement. Most likely, the eyes will not remain closed. The jaw will relax and drop, causing the mouth to remain open. Frequently, there will be subtle sounds or noises coming from the body due to the shifting of fluids and general internal changes. Please keep these changes in mind and be prepared as they may occur while you are present.

Again, there is no rush to do anything, but it would be very much appreciated if you would take a few minutes to step out of the room to make calls or get a breath of fresh air. This will allow the caregivers time to come in and respectfully do the care that is required and needs to be done after someone passes.

Please make sure the nurse has all the necessary information regarding the selected funeral home etc., as she will be making the call. There is no rush.

Take the time you need. Just let her know when you are ready to have the call made.

Some families may begin to pack up their loved ones belongings at this time, while others are not in an emotional state to do so. Let the staff know if you will be coming at a later time to collect their items. If you feel you are not able to pack the belongings yourself, let the staff know, and they will be happy to do that for you.

Some family members choose to remain with their loved one until the funeral home comes to transport. If this is the case, you need to be aware of what will take place. By law the deceased, must be contained in a closed unit for transport. This is usually a lined cloth bag. With the assistance of the staff, the body will be transferred from the bed to the opened cloth bag on the gurney. The bag will then be zipped from head to toe for transport. This can be very distressing for family members and loved ones to watch. It is okay ***not*** to stay. If you want to be of assistance and feel the need to serve, taking charge of your loved one's eye glasses, dentures or personal jewelry that is to go to the funeral home would be extremely helpful to the staff. Please let the nurse know what items you are taking so it can be documented in the patient's inventory list.

Self Care

Accompanying someone through the process of dying is extremely draining and exhausting for all involved. It takes its toll on our bodies, minds and spiritual health. It is important that you take care of yourself by proper nourishment and rest. The ordeal is hard enough without being on the verge of illness due to lack of sleep, and improper eating.

The days that follow the death of a loved one are demanding and will most always call for important decisions of some kind to be made. You will be better able to do this if you are well rested.

Summary

One to Three Months

Withdrawal

Increased sleep

Decreased appetite

Self-Preparation

Decreased communication

One to Two Weeks

Disorientation

Increased agitation

Talking with those we don’t see

Increased confusion

Terminal restlessness

Surge of energy

Physical Changes

Increased or decreased pulse

Color changes of the skin

Increased perspiration

Irregular respirations

Decreased blood pressure

Congestion

Change in body temperature

Increased sleep/coma

Little to no intake

Little to no urinary output

Days to Hours

Many or all of the signs and symptoms found in the one to two week period are intensified.

Surge of energy is possible

Extended periods of apnea

Mottling

Incontinent of bowel and / or bladder

Changes in the breathing pattern

Increased congestion

In the days that follow the passing of your loved one, take the time to find a quiet spot. "Be still" and you most likely will *feel* the persons presence or energy. As time passes and you continue to validate through prayer and witness to others the love and blessings that person brought into your life, it will become easier to feel their Spirit or energy around you. Always acknowledge them in your prayers and thank God for them. Remember, their Spirit is always with us and "it is never really ***goodbye***, it's till we meet again." May God always have His hand on you and bless you.

Do not stand at my grave and weep
I am not there, I do not sleep
I am a thousand winds that blow
I am the diamond's glint on snow
I am the sunlight on ripened grain
I am the autumn's gentle rain
When you awaken
In the morning's hush
I am the swift uplifting rush
Of quiet birds in circled flight
I am the soft stars
that shine at night
Do not stand by my grave and cry
I am not there
I did not die
I am with God loving you

Author unknown

Notes

Things to Do

Important Phone Numbers

Special Memories

Journal

God Bless You